CONTENTS

A SURPRISE ATTACK

December 7, 1941, was a quiet Sunday in Washington, DC. At the White House, President Franklin Delano Roosevelt was recovering from a cold. He ate lunch with his friend and adviser, Harry Hopkins. As they finished eating, Roosevelt's phone rang. US Secretary of the Navy Frank Knox was on the line. He had startling news. The Japanese had begun a surprise attack on US ships in Pearl Harbor, Hawaii.

Japanese airplanes bomb Pearl Harbor, Hawaii, on December 7, 1941.

Knox shared with Roosevelt the telegram he had received from Pearl Harbor. It said, "AIR RAID ON PEARL HARBOR—THIS IS NO DRILL." Hopkins thought it was probably incorrect information. Roosevelt was not so sure. He began to gather his cabinet and military leaders.

Meanwhile, Roosevelt's secretary, Grace Tully, was taking calls from the US Navy. Officers provided updates on the events at Pearl Harbor. Roosevelt was angry but remained calm. He shook his head sadly as more bad news arrived.

The worry and anger in the room grew. The military had been unprepared for the attack. In only one hour and 15 minutes, Japanese bombs and torpedoes had destroyed 169 airplanes. Nineteen ships had been sunk or damaged. More than 2,400 Americans had died.

The Call to War

The next day, Roosevelt spoke to the US Congress and the nation. He confirmed what many Americans feared: "Yesterday, December 7, 1941—a date which will live in infamy—the United States of America was suddenly and deliberately attacked by naval and air forces of the Empire of Japan."

Just minutes after Roosevelt's speech, Congress declared war on Japan. The United States was about to enter the biggest war of the century—one it had spent years trying to avoid.

STAYING NEUTRAL

The attack on Pearl Harbor occurred more than two years into World War II (1939–1945). The attack came as a surprise to many Americans. But the war had been raging for years. Americans watched the war develop in Europe in the late 1930s. They knew Germany's leader, Adolf Hitler, wanted to expand Germany's power. He planned to do it by taking over nearby countries.

Adolf Hitler had been building power in Germany throughout the 1930s.

9

On September 1, 1939, war broke out when Germany invaded Poland. France and the United Kingdom joined Poland in fighting against Germany two days later.

Most Americans wanted to stay out of the war. Memories of World War I (1914–1918) were fresh in their minds. Many US soldiers had died in the war. It had also been expensive. Many nations had not yet repaid their war loans to the United States. A poll in 1939 showed that 94 percent

Americans protest against joining World War II in 1939.

of Americans wanted to stay out of the new war in Europe.

Roosevelt also wanted to stay neutral. On September 3, 1939, he spoke to the American people over the radio. "This nation will remain a neutral nation," he said. "I have said not once but many times that I have seen war and that I hate war."

Roosevelt signs a bill agreeing to send supplies to warring nations.

Cash and Carry

Despite his wish to stay out of the war, Roosevelt knew Hitler had to be stopped. Roosevelt wanted to help France and the United Kingdom without sending troops. He thought sending supplies was the next best thing. If he could help these countries defeat the Germans, no Americans would need to go to war.

Roosevelt spoke to the US Congress about this idea. After much debate, Congress allowed the United States to sell supplies to nations at war. But the nations had to pay in cash and carry the supplies on their own ships.

The plan worked well. But Roosevelt knew he needed to do more. He worried that the United States was unprepared. The US army was only the 17th largest in the world. To improve this, starting in 1939, Roosevelt greatly increased the country's defense budget. It was

Fireside Chats

Between March 1933 and June 1944, Roosevelt addressed the nation 30 times through what became known as fireside chats. These speeches were broadcast to the nation over the radio. In them, Roosevelt spoke directly to the American people about problems facing the nation. Many Americans found hope and comfort by listening to the president speak openly about important issues.

the largest amount ever spent on the military while the country was at peace.

In the meantime, Germany was growing stronger. It had joined two other world powers, Japan and Italy. The three nations became known as the Axis Powers. In September 1940, they signed the Tripartite Pact. They agreed to stand together during the war. They also agreed to attack the United States if it got in the way of their plans to conquer other lands.

A Third Term

In the midst of this, the United States was set to hold a presidential election. Roosevelt was not sure he wanted to run for a third term. But he felt a sense of duty toward the war in Europe. With this in mind, he agreed to run for a third term. During his campaign, Roosevelt continued to promise that the United States would stay out of the war.

With the threat of war looming, Americans did not want to change leaders. Roosevelt easily defeated his opponent, Wendell Willkie, in the election of November 1940. Roosevelt was the first president in US history to serve for a third term. He was experienced. But the coming years would test Roosevelt's leadership skills in every way.

EXPLORE ONLINE

Chapter Two quotes Roosevelt's fireside chat from September 3, 1939. The website below provides an audio recording of the speech. Listen to the recording as if you were an American listening to it on the radio in 1939. How does Roosevelt try to reassure the American people? Why do you think fireside chats worked so well?

Fireside Chat 14: On the European War
mycorelibrary.com/franklin-delano-roosevelt

CHAPTER THREE

ARSENAL OF DEMOCRACY

Throughout the 1940 presidential campaign, the situation in Europe had grown more dangerous. After Germany had control of Poland, German troops moved to conquer other nations. By June 1940, Germany had taken France. The United Kingdom was now the last country standing in the battle against Germany's military.

German troops march through Paris, France, in August 1940.

A German bomber flies over London in the fall of 1940.

That same summer, Germany began attacking the United Kingdom. At first German planes bombed aircraft factories, radar towers, and airfields. Then, in September, German aircraft began targeting London. For 57 nights in a row, German bombs thundered down on the city. The British stood their ground. They shot down German planes faster than they could be made.

By the winter of 1940, the United Kingdom had successfully defended itself against Germany. But the bombings had left the country's military weak and nearly out of money. British leaders were not sure whether they could defend against another German attack. Roosevelt knew what this meant. If Germany seized the United Kingdom, the Axis Powers would control Europe, Asia, Africa, and Australia.

The Lend-Lease Act

Roosevelt thought the best way to prevent the Axis Powers from taking worldwide control was to help the United Kingdom. If the British could defeat the Axis Powers in Europe, then US troops would not need to fight. The United Kingdom's leader, Winston Churchill, told Roosevelt, "Give us the tools, and we will finish the job."

In March 1941, Congress passed Roosevelt's plan to aid the United Kingdom. It was called the Lend-Lease Act. It let the United States sell, lend, or lease tanks, airplanes, ammunition, and other supplies to its allies. Many Americans were against

Winston Churchill

On the day the United Kingdom declared war on Germany in 1939, Winston Churchill took a post in the British government as head of the navy. Roosevelt sent him a telegram of congratulations. It was the start of a close friendship between the two men.

Churchill became the United Kingdom's prime minister in 1940. He and Roosevelt were united by their desire to defeat the Axis Powers. Churchill later wrote, "To have the United States at our side was to me the greatest joy." Churchill and Roosevelt worked well together. This gave the two countries a great advantage in the war.

this program. They feared it would lead the country into the war.

By the spring of 1941, Hitler controlled nearly all of Europe. German troops were preparing to invade Libya, Egypt, and the Soviet Union. Roosevelt worried Hitler would soon want to conquer North America. The war was no longer only a problem in Europe. It was now the world's problem.

Roosevelt began to prepare Americans for the possibility of war. On May 27, 1941, he spoke to the nation. "Nobody can

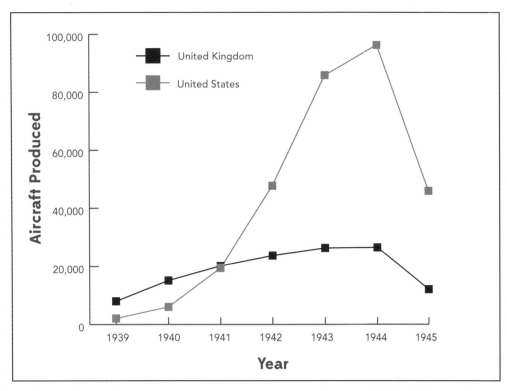

Aircraft Production
This chart tracks US and British aircraft production starting in 1939. What do you notice about each country's production over time? How does seeing the information help you think about US involvement in the war differently?

foretell tonight just when the acts of the dictators will ripen into attack on this hemisphere and us," he said. "But we know enough by now to realize that it would be suicide to wait until they are in our front yard."

Later that summer, Roosevelt and Churchill planned a secret meeting. In August 1941, they

The Holocaust

As the Nazi Party gained more power in Germany, the Holocaust began. Nazis gathered Jews from Poland, Germany, and elsewhere into camps. The conditions were terrible. People lived in dirty, crowded rooms. Some were forced to do hard labor. The prisoners did not get enough food. In 1942 Nazis began loading Jews onto trains. The trains went to extermination camps. In these camps, Jews were forced into gas chambers, where they were killed. More than 6 million Jews had died by the end of the war.

Nazis also targeted other groups, such as Polish people and disabled people. Approximately 5 million non-Jews died in the Holocaust.

met aboard the USS *Augusta* off the coast of Newfoundland. The result was the Atlantic Charter. In it the leaders promised to seek peace after Germany was defeated. They also promised to disarm any nations unsettling the peace.

Trouble in the Pacific

Until this point, Roosevelt's focus had been on stopping Germany. But other Axis Powers were also at work. Japan had been trying to take parts of Asia for years. The country

Roosevelt and Churchill discuss the Atlantic Charter on a ship off the coast of Newfoundland.

controlled parts of China. And in July 1941, it seized control of Indochina, a region that includes present-day Vietnam. Roosevelt was angry another Axis Power was claiming more land. He decided to stop US trade with Japan.

Japan had received 80 percent of its oil from the United States. Japan could not carry out its military plans without oil. On September 6, Japan's leaders threatened war against the United States and the United Kingdom if a trade agreement was not reached.

Japanese commander Yamamoto Isoroku planned the surprise attack on Pearl Harbor.

Roosevelt and Japanese leaders negotiated for months. Roosevelt wanted Japan to reject the Tripartite Pact with Germany and Italy. He also wanted Japan's troops to leave other parts of Asia. The Japanese refused both demands. On November 26, the Japanese cut off trade talks.

Japanese military commander Yamamoto Isoroku began to create a plan. He wanted to carry out a surprise attack on US ships at Pearl Harbor, Hawaii. Yamamoto's plans went into action on the morning of December 7, 1941. The United States had finally been drawn into World War II.

On December 29, 1940, Roosevelt delivered a fireside chat about US involvement in the war:

Frankly and definitely there is danger ahead—danger against which we must prepare. But we well know that we cannot escape danger, or the fear of danger, by crawling into bed and pulling the covers over our heads. . . . I want to make it clear that it is the purpose of the nation to build now with all possible speed every machine, every arsenal, every factory that we need to manufacture our defense material. We have the men, the skill, the wealth, and above all, the will. . . . We must be the great arsenal of democracy. For us this is an emergency as serious as war itself. We must apply ourselves to our task with the same resolution, the same sense of urgency, the same spirit of patriotism and sacrifice as we would show were we at war.

Source: Franklin Roosevelt. "On National Security." FDR Presidential Library and Museum. *Marist College, September 15, 2009. Web. Accessed June 24, 2015.*

Changing Minds

How does Roosevelt speak to Americans who want to stay neutral? If you were in favor of neutrality, would this speech change your mind? What does Roosevelt say to inspire Americans to action?

CHAPTER FOUR

JOINING THE FIGHT

Americans were outraged upon hearing about the Pearl Harbor attack. Many wanted the United States to join the war because American lives had been lost. On the morning of Monday, December 8, 1941, President Roosevelt signed a declaration of war against Japan. Germany declared war on the United States in response. Roosevelt then

Roosevelt asks Congress for a declaration of war against Japan on December 8, 1941.

Churchill, *center left*, and Roosevelt, *center right*, wait for a car outside the White House in December 1941.

signed a declaration of war against Germany on December 11.

Roosevelt was now leading a nation at war. He invited Churchill to the White House to plan. Churchill arrived on December 22. He stayed in a room down the hall from Roosevelt for the next month. During that time, they created the plan they hoped would bring an end to the war. The two nations became known as the Allied Powers. Other nations later joined the Allies.

The first decision the Allied leaders had to make was whether to fight Germany or Japan first. Many

Americans wanted to first fight Japan. They wanted revenge for the attack on Pearl Harbor. Churchill and Roosevelt did not think this was the best plan. Instead they chose to fight Germany first. They thought Germany was more powerful. Its strength made it a bigger threat to the world.

The Germany-first plan was in place. But the Allies still had much work ahead of them. Neither the United States nor the British military was ready for action. The United Kingdom's forces had been weakened by the war. The US military was also unprepared, despite Roosevelt's early efforts.

Preparing for War

Roosevelt and Churchill realized they needed to build up their troops and supplies. Roosevelt spoke to the nation in January 1942. He said, "We must convert every available plant and tool to war production. . . . Our workers stand ready to work long hours; to turn out more in a day's work; to keep the wheels turning and the fires burning."

Executive Order 9066

After Japan attacked Pearl Harbor, fear and prejudice spread across the country. People worried that Japanese Americans might be spies. Many Japanese Americans were US citizens. Some were veterans of the US military. But on February 19, 1942, Roosevelt reacted to pressure from his advisers. He signed Executive Order 9066. It allowed the US military to relocate anyone thought to be a threat. The military forced Japanese Americans on the West Coast to move to fenced-in camps. The camps eventually held more than 110,000 people. Many Japanese Americans lost property and jobs because of the order. The last camp closed in March 1946.

With those words, Roosevelt started the largest wartime production in US history. Twenty-four million Americans began working for the war effort. Every industry was involved. Car factories began making aircraft. Factories that once made nails began producing ammunition clips. The plan was successful. By 1942 American factories were completing an average of one bomber per hour and a jeep every two minutes.

Meanwhile, Roosevelt was working on secret

plans. He had approved the creation of an atomic bomb at the start of the war. Scientists thought the bomb could destroy an entire city. No other nation had made an atomic bomb. Roosevelt wanted the powerful weapon in his arsenal.

The D-day Invasion

Roosevelt kept in close contact with Churchill. In November 1943, the two leaders met in Tehran, Iran, to go over their war plans. This time the Soviet Union's leader, Joseph Stalin, joined them. Stalin wanted to end Germany's attacks on his country. He wanted Allied troops to start their attack quickly. In exchange, Stalin promised to send Soviet troops to fight Japan once Germany was beaten.

By mid-1944 the US and British militaries were finally ready for their big attack against German forces. The operation was nicknamed D-day. It began on June 6, 1944. That day Allied troops traveled across the English Channel and landed on the beaches of Normandy, France.

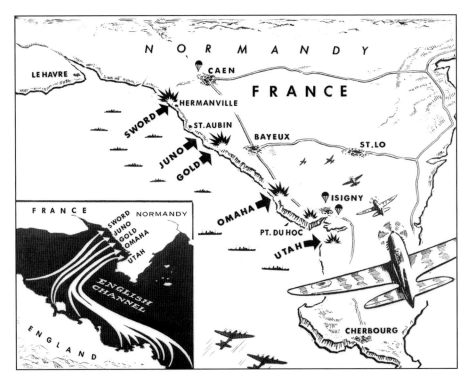

Map of the Normandy Invasion

This map illustrates where troops landed and were dropped during the invasion of Normandy, France. How does seeing the map help you think about the operation differently?

France was freed from German control within two months. US and British troops continued to march across Europe. They freed other countries Germany had taken over. By the winter of 1944, US and British forces controlled most of Europe. The Germany-first strategy had worked. Now the Allies were ready to turn their attention to the Pacific.

On June 6, 1944, Roosevelt spoke to Americans over the radio. He discussed the D-day invasion for the first time. It had been top secret until that time. He then led the nation in prayer.

My fellow Americans: Last night, when I spoke with you about the fall of Rome, I knew at that moment that troops of the United States and our allies were crossing the Channel in another and greater operation. It has come to pass with success thus far.

And so, in this poignant hour, I ask you to join with me in prayer:

Almighty God: Our sons, pride of our nation, this day have set upon a mighty endeavor, a struggle to preserve our republic, our religion, and our civilization, and to set free a suffering humanity. Lead them straight and true; give strength to their arms, stoutness to their hearts, steadfastness in their faith.

Source: Franklin Roosevelt. "Prayer on D-Day." FDR Presidential Library and Museum. Marist College, September 15, 2009. Web. Accessed June 24, 2015.

Consider Your Audience

How did Roosevelt try to connect with Americans in this speech? How would you share difficult news such as this if you were president?

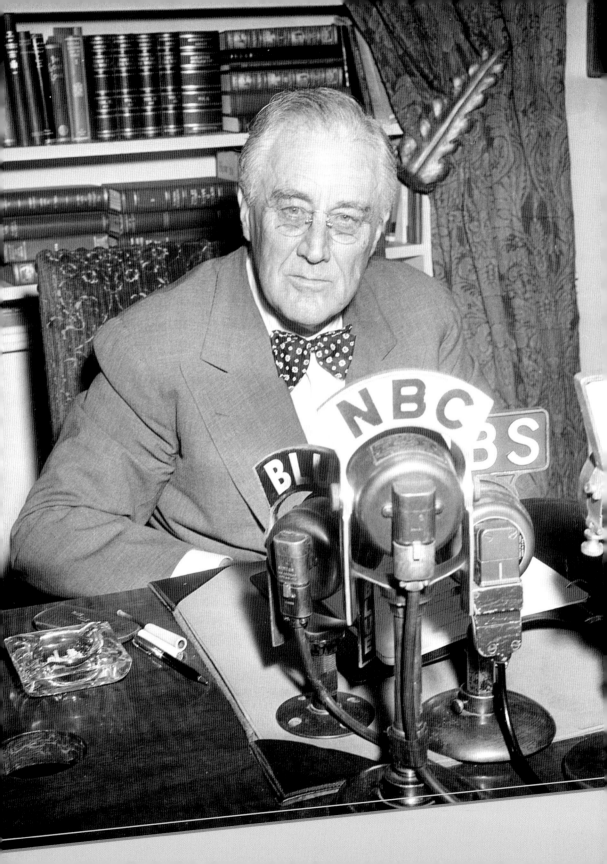

THE END
OF AN ERA

The war years had been long and difficult for Roosevelt. The stress began to show in his health. He was less involved in war planning than he had been earlier. He spent much of his time resting in bed. Doctors discovered Roosevelt was suffering from heart problems.

Despite these problems, he felt he had a duty to continue on as president and return the United States

Roosevelt prepares to address the nation during a fireside chat in June 1944.

Churchill, Roosevelt, and Stalin meet at the Yalta Conference. At the conference, the leaders discussed plans for after the war.

to peace. Roosevelt ran for a fourth term as president in November 1944. No US president had ever done so before. Roosevelt campaigned hard and was able to convince voters he was healthy enough to continue as president. Once again, Americans were unwilling to change leaders while at war. Roosevelt won a fourth term.

Roosevelt again met with Churchill and Stalin in February 1945. Their meeting was at Yalta, Crimea. They met to plan the war's end. They planned to separate Germany into four zones. The United States, France, the United Kingdom, and the Soviet Union would each control one zone. The Soviet Union would also control Poland. Stalin promised he would allow Poland to elect its own leaders.

Roosevelt was not pleased with the talks with Stalin. The Soviet leader's troops were strong. And they were positioned throughout Eastern Europe. Roosevelt feared Stalin would go back on his word and seize the region. After the conference, he told one of his aides, "I didn't say the result was good. I said it was the best I could do."

Last Days

Roosevelt returned home thin, weak, and tired. He was unable to stand when he spoke to Congress about the Yalta Conference. In late March, he traveled to Warm Springs, Georgia, to celebrate Easter and rest. While sitting in his cottage, he suffered a stroke. He died on April 12, 1945. Harry S. Truman became the next US president later that day.

Roosevelt's work in leading the United States through the war was almost complete when Truman took office. In Europe a peace treaty went into effect on May 8, 1945, less than a month after Roosevelt's death. But fighting in the Pacific continued. Truman knew he must end it quickly.

Truman used Roosevelt's secret weapon: the atomic bomb. He believed using the weapon would spare American lives and end the war sooner. On August 6, he gave orders to drop an atomic bomb on Hiroshima, Japan. Americans dropped another atomic bomb three days later on Nagasaki, Japan. The bombs killed nearly 140,000 people.

The War's End

The Soviet Union declared war on Japan in the days between the two bombings. This was what Stalin had promised Roosevelt and Churchill two years earlier during their talks in Iran. The devastation of the atomic bombs and the Soviet attacks led Japanese leaders to seek peace. On August 14, 1945, Japan agreed to surrender.

The war Roosevelt had tried so hard to avoid was finally over. Japan surrendered less than five months after his death. Roosevelt's commitment to peace is still present today. His work with Churchill and Stalin led to the creation of the United Nations. This organization began in October 1945. It still meets today with 193 member nations. They meet to discuss problems and maintain peace. The group also

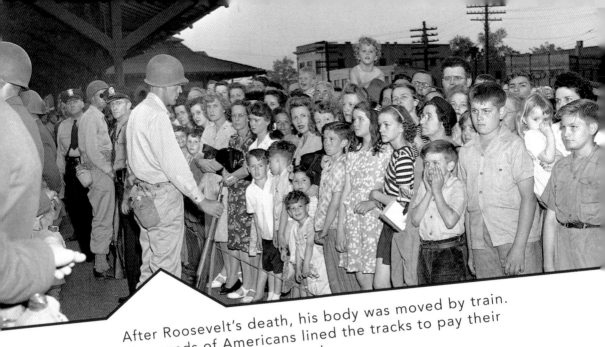

After Roosevelt's death, his body was moved by train. Thousands of Americans lined the tracks to pay their respects as the train passed.

upholds international laws, works for human rights, and encourages social progress.

Some of Roosevelt's work was not so successful, though. The deal he and Churchill made with Stalin in Yalta ended badly. Stalin took control of Eastern Europe even though he had promised not to. He wanted to keep Germany from attacking the Soviet Union again.

The disagreements between the Soviet Union and the United States became intense. Both nations threatened each other with atomic weapons. These tensions were called the Cold War. It lasted until 1991, when the Soviet Union collapsed.

Despite his role in setting up the Cold War, Roosevelt is remembered as one of the greatest US presidents. Americans relied on his openness and confidence as a leader throughout World War II. His close friendship with Churchill helped create the Allied Powers. And Roosevelt's plan to develop the atomic bomb brought about the war's end. His four terms shaped the course of the United States and is still felt today.

FURTHER EVIDENCE

Roosevelt's Legacy

Chapter Five covers Roosevelt's death and legacy. What was one of the chapter's main points? What evidence supports it? The article at the website below discusses Roosevelt's legacy. What in the article supports Chapter Five's main point?

Roosevelt's Legacy

mycorelibrary.com/franklin-delano-roosevelt

IMPORTANT DATES

Sept. 1939

World War II begins when Germany invades Poland.

June 1940

Germany controls France and begins attacking the United Kingdom.

Sept. 1940

Germany, Italy, and Japan sign the Tripartite Pact.

Nov. 1943

Roosevelt, Churchill, and Stalin meet in Tehran, Iran.

June 1944

The Allies launch the D-day invasion.

Feb. 1945

Roosevelt, Churchill, and Stalin meet at Yalta.

Mar. 1941

Congress passes the Lend-Lease Act.

Aug. 1941

Roosevelt and Churchill create the Atlantic Charter.

Dec. 1941

Japan attacks Pearl Harbor, Hawaii.

April 1945

Roosevelt dies.

May 1945

Germany surrenders to the Allies.

Aug. 1945

Japan surrenders to the Allies.

STOP AND THINK

Why Do I Care?

In the late 1930s, most Americans believed World War II was Europe's problem. That changed after Japan's attack on Pearl Harbor, Hawaii. Americans still fiercely debate involvement in foreign wars. Why should or why shouldn't Americans be involved in international conflicts? What are the benefits of staying neutral? What are the risks of being neutral?

Another View

Americans were surprised by the attack on Pearl Harbor. Some people, however, believe Roosevelt knew Japan was going to attack Pearl Harbor. They believe he let it happen so the United States would have a reason to be involved in the war. Ask an adult to help you find an article about this topic. What evidence supports the theory that Roosevelt had advance information about the attack? What evidence supports the theory that he did not?

Take a Stand

Chapter Four mentions Roosevelt's consent to develop an atomic bomb. Dropping atomic bombs ended the war, which many people welcomed. But the new weapon created a rush among nations to create atomic bombs. Do you think Roosevelt was right to support the creation of an atomic bomb? Why?

You Are There

Imagine you are a sailor aboard the USS *Augusta* when Roosevelt and Churchill sign the Atlantic Charter in 1941. Write a journal entry describing the scene. How do you feel, as a sailor, knowing war is nearing?

GLOSSARY

allies
nations that agree to work together for a common purpose

arsenal
a collection of stored weapons

atomic bomb
a weapon that creates a massive explosion when the atoms in the bomb's fuel are split

cabinet
a group of advisers to the president

campaign
a series of events that show the public a candidate's skills and beliefs

disarm
to remove weapons from a person or group

lease
to lend an item for a specific rate and period of time

neutral
not taking sides in a fight

LEARN MORE

Books

Adams, Simon. *World War II*. New York: DK Publishing, 2014.

Gunderson, Megan M. *Franklin D. Roosevelt*. Edina, MN: Abdo Publishing, 2009.

Hamilton, John. *World War II: Leaders and Generals*. Edina, MN: Abdo Publishing, 2012.

Websites

To learn more about Presidential Perspectives, visit **booklinks.abdopublishing.com**. These links are routinely monitored and updated to provide the most current information available.

Visit **mycorelibrary.com** for free additional tools for teachers and students.

INDEX

ABOUT THE AUTHOR

Kate Conley has written and edited many books for young readers. She lives in Minnesota with her husband and two children.